English
Through
GrammarStories
1A

Steven J. Molinsky
Bill Bliss

Illustrated by
Richard E. Hill

Prentice Hall Regents, Englewood Cliffs, NJ 07632

Library of Congress Cataloging in Publication Data
(Revised for Book 1A)

MOLINSKY, STEVEN J.
    Line by line.

    Includes index.
    1. English language—Textbooks for foreign speakers.
I. Bliss, Bill. II. Title.
PE1128.M68 1983b   428.6′4   83-9771
ISBN 0-13-537092-2 (Book 1A)

Editorial production/supervision: Dan Mausner
Cover design: Suzanne Behnke
Page layout: Margaret Mary Finnerty
Manufacturing buyer: Harry P. Baisley

Printed in the United States of America

10 9

ISBN 0-13-537092-2

PRENTICE-HALL INTERNATIONAL, INC., *London*
PRENTICE-HALL OF AUSTRALIA PTY. LIMITED, *Sydney*
EDITORA PRENTICE-HALL DO BRASIL, LTDA., *Rio de Janeiro*
PRENTICE-HALL CANADA INC., *Toronto*
PRENTICE-HALL OF INDIA PRIVATE LIMITED, *New Delhi*
PRENTICE-HALL OF JAPAN, INC., *Tokyo*
PRENTICE-HALL OF SOUTHEAST ASIA PTE. LTD., *Singapore*
WHITEHALL BOOKS LIMITED, *Wellington, New Zealand*

Contents

To the Teacher

Line By Line is a collection of "GrammarStories"—reading selections which are designed to provide meaningful, relevant, and enjoyable reading practice while offering a clear, intensive focus on specific aspects of English grammar. Each chapter provides reading and writing reinforcement of the structures and vocabulary presented in the corresponding chapter of our textbook, *Side By Side: English Grammar Through Guided Conversations*. *Line By Line* can be used in conjunction with *Side By Side* or independently as a separate reading and writing text.

All components of *Line By Line* have been designed to offer students opportunities for true interactive communicative practice in the language classroom. The stories in the text are brief; we have tried to create characters and situations that are simple and straightforward, while highlighting specific grammatical structures. The extensive illustrations serve as visual cues that guide learners through the reading selections. Follow-up questions, coupled with these illustrations, form the basis for student discussion and retelling of the stories. A feature of each chapter is the "In Your Own Words" activity, which gives students an opportunity to create original stories based on their interests, backgrounds, and imaginations.

Suggestions for Using *LINE BY LINE*

Previewing a GrammarStory

Some teachers might want to preview each story either by briefly setting the scene or by having students talk about the illustrations or guess the content of the story from the title. Some teachers may also find it useful to introduce new vocabulary items before they are encountered in the story. (A chapter-by-chapter word list can be found in the back of the book.)

Other teachers may prefer to skip this previewing step, and instead have their students experience the subject matter and any unfamiliar words in the context of the initial reading of the story.

Reading and Talking About a Story

There are many ways in which students can read and talk about the stories. We don't want to dictate any specific procedures. Rather, we encourage you to use strategies that are compatible with the needs and abilities of your students as well as your own teaching style.

For the initial reading, students can read silently to themselves or follow along as the story is told by the teacher, one or more students, or the narrator on the tape. Some teachers might want to repeat this step before moving on.

After this initial reading, a teacher might want to check students' understanding of new vocabulary items and ask students if they have any questions about what they have read.

The questions after each story serve to check students' comprehension and offer practice with the specific grammatical structures. The questions also serve as a springboard for classroom interaction by offering students a framework for discussing the story's content and characters.

The questions can be used in several ways. They might be read aloud by the teacher or students or read silently from the book. Students may answer them with their books open as they scan the text or refer to the illustrations, or with books closed.

Pair practice or small group work can also be effective for talking about the story. Students can work with one or more partners and take turns asking and answering the questions. This form of practice can serve as a prelude to a full-class discussion of the story.

Questions can also be answered in writing either in class or at home. Teachers will find that using the questions in this way not only offers written practice, but also helps students focus more clearly on the grammatical structures highlighted in each chapter.

By writing out the answers for homework, students will be better prepared to discuss and retell a story in class the next day. However, we discourage students from actually referring to their written answers during discussion so that the classroom conversation can be as interactive as possible.

Retelling a Story

The way in which the stories are written and the illustrations that accompany them enable students to retell them with little difficulty. Teachers find retelling to be a useful activity for reviewing the content of a story and the grammar it contains, or for providing additional speaking and pronunciation practice. In retelling stories, students should refer to the illustrations, which usually offer clues to story content, characters, and sequence of action.

There are several approaches for retelling stories. One student might retell the entire story in front of the class; students might work in pairs, retelling the story to each other and perhaps then presenting the story to the class; or students may retell it as a "circle story," with one student beginning with the first line, another contributing the second line, and so on.

Students do not have to retell the stories exactly as they appear in the book. They can adapt, paraphrase, or add to the story as they wish.

Many stories are appropriate for role-play activities. Students can play the roles of different characters, creating speaking lines and acting out the situations. One student might be assigned as the narrator to explain the action taking place. Other students, in the audience, can "interview" the actors, asking them who they are, what they're doing, and how they feel about what's happening.

"In Your Own Words"

The "In Your Own Words" activity in each chapter is designed to guide students in their creation of original stories. Students are asked to tell about such topics as their homes, schools, jobs, friends, families, and themselves.

Teachers should go over the instructions for the activities and make sure that their students understand what is expected. Students should then write their stories, taking sufficient time to think about what they want to say, and use a dictionary for any new words they wish to include. These activities are perhaps most appropriately assigned for homework to guarantee that all students will have sufficient time to develop their ideas and write them out.

Many teachers will find these written pieces a basis for effective peer work among the students. Students can work together, telling their stories to each other, asking and answering questions about the stories, and correcting each other's written work.

As a final step, the "In Your Own Words" activities serve as a vehicle for classroom speaking practice. Students can tell their own stories, or perhaps tell the stories of their "peer work" partners, while the rest of the class listens and asks questions.

In conclusion, we have attempted to help students develop their reading and writing abilities in English through a collection of carefully structured stories that are both lighthearted in content and relevant to students' lives. While we hope that we have conveyed to you the substance of our textbook, we also hope that we have conveyed the spirit: that the study of reading and writing can be dynamic . . . communicative . . . and fun.

Steven J. Molinsky
Bill Bliss

To Be: Introduction

What's Your Name?

What's Your Name?

My name is David Miller. I'm American. I'm from New York.

My name is Mrs. White. My phone number is 237-5976.

My name is Susan Black. My address is 378 Main Street, Waterville, Florida. My license number is 112897.

My name is Mr. Taylor. My apartment number is 3-B.

My name is William Chen. My address is 694 River Street, New York City. My telephone number is 469-7750. My Social Security number is 044-35-9862.

Fill out the form below.

ACME COMPANY

Name _____

Address _____

_____

Telephone Number _____

**To Be + Location
Subject Pronouns**

The Students
in My English Class
All the Students
in My English Class
Are Absent Today

The Students in My English Class

The students in my English class are very interesting.

Henry is Chinese. He's from Shanghai.

Natasha is Russian. She's from Leningrad.

Mr. and Mrs. Ramirez are Puerto Rican.
They're from San Juan.

George is Greek. He's from Athens.

Nicole is French. She's from Paris.

Mr. and Mrs. Sato are Japanese.
They're from Tokyo.

My friend Maria and I are Mexican.
We're from Mexico City.

Yes, the students in my English class are very interesting.
We're from many different countries . . . and we're friends.

1. What nationality is Henry?
   Where is he from?
2. What nationality is Natasha?
   Where is she from?
3. What nationality are Mr. and Mrs. Ramirez?
   Where are they from?
4. What nationality is George?
   Where is he from?
5. What nationality is Nicole?
   Where is she from?
6. What nationality are Mr. and Mrs. Sato?
   Where are they from?
7. What nationality are Maria and I?
   Where are we from?

8. *Tell about the students in* YOUR *English class.*
   Where are they from?

George

Maria

Mr. and Mrs. Sato

our English teacher

All the Students in My English Class
Are Absent Today

All the students in my English class are absent today.

George is absent.
He's in the hospital.

Maria is absent.
She's at the dentist.

Mr. and Mrs. Sato are absent.
They're at the Social Security office.

Even our English teacher is absent.
He's home in bed!

What a shame! Everybody in my English class is absent today. Everybody except me.

    1. Where's George?
    2. Where's Maria?
    3. Where are Mr. and Mrs. Sato?
    4. Where's our English teacher?

Tell about YOUR English class.

Which students are in class today?
Which students are absent today?
Where are they?

**Present Continuous
Tense**

In the Park
At Home in the Yard

In the Park

The Jones family is in the park today. The sun is shining and the birds are singing. It's a beautiful day!

Mr. Jones is reading the newspaper. Mrs. Jones is listening to the radio. Sally and Patty Jones are studying. And Tommy Jones is playing the guitar.

The Jones family is very happy today. It's a beautiful day and they're in the park.

1. Where's the Jones family today?
2. What's Mr. Jones doing?
3. What's Mrs. Jones doing?
4. What are Sally and Patty Jones doing?
5. What's Tommy Jones doing?

At Home in the Yard

The Smith family is at home in the yard today. The sun is shining and the birds are singing. It's a beautiful day!

Mr. Smith is planting flowers. Mrs. Smith is drinking lemonade and reading a book. Mary and Billy Smith are playing with the dog. And Sam Smith is sleeping.

The Smith family is very happy today. It's a beautiful day and they're at home in the yard.

1. Where's the Smith family today?
2. What's Mr. Smith doing?
3. What's Mrs. Smith doing?
4. What are Mary and Billy Smith doing?
5. What's Sam Smith doing?

At the Beach

The Martinez family is at the beach today. Using the picture below, tell a story about the Martinez family.

Possessive Adjectives

A Busy Day

A Busy Day

Everybody at 149 River Street is very busy today.

Mr. Anderson is cleaning his apartment. Mrs. Wilson is fixing her kitchen sink. Mr. and Mrs. Thomas are painting their living room. Mrs. Black is doing her exercises. Tommy Lee is feeding his dog. And Mr. and Mrs. Lane are washing their car.

I'm busy, too. I'm washing my windows . . . and of course, I'm watching all my neighbors.

It's a very busy day at 149 River Street.

1. What's Mr. Anderson doing?
2. What's Mrs. Wilson doing?
3. What are Mr. and Mrs. Thomas doing?
4. What's Mrs. Black doing?
5. What's Tommy Lee doing?
6. What are Mr. and Mrs. Lane doing?
7. What am I doing?

A Busy Day

Everybody at 210 Main Street is very busy today. Using the picture below, tell a story about them.

Adjectives

Dear Mother

Dear Mother

Dear Mother,

I'm writing to you from our hotel at Sludge Beach. Ralph and I are on vacation with the children for a few days. We're happy to be here, but to tell the truth, we're having a few problems.

The weather isn't very good. In fact, it's cold and cloudy. Right now I'm looking out the window and it's raining cats and dogs.

The children aren't very happy. In fact, they're bored and they're having a terrible time. Right now they're sitting on the bed, playing cards and watching TV.

The restaurants here are expensive, and the food isn't very good. In fact, Ralph is at the doctor's office right now. He's having problems with his stomach.

All the other hotels here are beautiful and new. Our hotel is ugly, and it's very, very old. In fact, right now a repairman is in our bathroom fixing the toilet.

As you can see, Mother, we're having a few problems here at Sludge Beach, but we're happy. We're happy to be on vacation, and we're happy to be together.

See you soon.

Love,

Ethel

1. Where are Ethel and Ralph?
2. How's the weather at Sludge Beach?
3. Is it raining?
4. Are the children happy?
5. What are they doing?
6. Tell about the restaurants at Sludge Beach.
7. Where's Ralph?
8. Why?
9. Tell about the other hotels at Sludge Beach.
10. Is Ethel and Ralph's hotel beautiful and new?
11. Ethel and Ralph are having a few problems on their vacation, but they're happy. Why?

Write a letter to a friend about your English class.

Dear _____,

    Let me tell you about my new English class. Our English teacher is _____. The students in our English class are very _____. The questions in our English book are very _____. The classroom is _____ and the school building is _____.

    I'm having a _____ time in my English class. Write back soon.

                    Sincerely,

                    _____

Here are some words you can use in your letter.

bad	handsome	noisy
beautiful	happy	old
big	heavy	quiet
clean	intelligent	small
cold	interesting	smart
difficult	large	terrible
easy	little	thin
friendly	new	ugly
good	nice	warm
		young

To Be: Review

Arthur Is Very Angry
Tom's Wedding Day

Arthur Is Very Angry

It's late at night. Arthur is sitting on his bed and he's looking at his clock. His neighbors are making a lot of noise, and Arthur is VERY angry.

The people in Apartment 2 are dancing. The man in Apartment 3 is vacuuming the carpet in his living room. The woman in Apartment 4 is practicing the violin. The teenagers in Apartment 5 are listening to loud rock music. The dog in Apartment 6 is barking. And the people in Apartment 7 are having a big argument.

It's very late and Arthur is tired and angry. What a terrible night!

1. What's Arthur doing?
2. Is he happy?
3. Why not?
4. What are the people in Apartment 2 doing?
5. What's the man in Apartment 3 doing?
6. What's the woman in Apartment 4 doing?
7. What are the teenagers in Apartment 5 doing?
8. What's the dog in Apartment 6 doing?
9. What are the people in Apartment 7 doing?

Tom's Wedding Day

Today is a very special day. It's my wedding day, and all my family and friends are here. Everybody is having a wonderful time.

My wife Jane is standing in front of the fireplace. She's wearing a beautiful white wedding gown. Uncle Harry is taking her photograph, and Aunt Emma is crying. (She's very sentimental.)

The band is playing my favorite popular music. My mother is dancing with Jane's father, and Jane's mother is dancing with my father.

My sister and Jane's brother are standing in the yard, eating wedding cake and talking about politics.

Our grandparents are sitting in the corner, drinking champagne and talking about "the good old days."

Everybody is having a good time. People are singing, dancing, and laughing, and our families are getting to know each other.

It's a very special day.

1. What day is today?
2. Where's Jane?
3. What's she wearing?
4. What's Uncle Harry doing?
5. What's Aunt Emma doing? Why?
6. What are Tom and Jane's parents doing?
7. What are his sister and her brother doing?
8. What are their grandparents doing?

Jennifer's Birthday Party

Today is a very special day. It's Jennifer's birthday party, and all her family and friends are there. Using the picture below, tell a story about her party.

**Prepositions
There Is/There Are**

The New Shopping Mall
Jane's Apartment Building

The New Shopping Mall

Everybody in Brewster is talking about the city's new shopping mall. The mall is outside the city, next to the Brewster airport. There are more than one hundred stores in the mall.

There are two big department stores. There are many clothing stores for men, women, and children. There's a very big toy store. There are two shoe stores, two drugstores, and four restaurants. There's even a movie theater.

Almost all the people in Brewster are happy that their city's new shopping mall is now open. But some people aren't happy.

The owners of the small stores in the old center of town are very upset. They're upset because there aren't many people shopping in their stores in the center of town. They're all shopping at the new mall.

1. What's everybody talking about?
2. Where's the mall?
3. What's in the mall?
4. Who isn't happy about the new mall?
5. Why?

Jane's Apartment Building

Jane's apartment building is in the center of town. Jane is very happy there because the building is in a very convenient place.

Across from the building, there's a laundromat, a bank, and a post office. Next to the building, there's a drugstore and a restaurant. Around the corner from the building, there are two gas stations.

There's a lot of noise near Jane's apartment building. There are a lot of cars on the street, and there are a lot of people walking on the sidewalk all day and all night.

Jane isn't very upset about the noise, though. Her building is in the center of town. It's a very busy place, but for Jane, it's a very convenient place to live.

1. Where's Jane's apartment building?
2. Why is Jane very happy there?
3. What's across from the building?
4. What's next to the building?
5. What's around the corner from the building?
6. Is Jane's neighborhood quiet? Why not?
7. Is Jane upset about the noise? Why not?

8. *Tell about YOUR neighborhood.*
   Is it convenient? Is it very busy?

George's Apartment Building

George's apartment building is in the center of town. George is very happy there because the building is in a very convenient place. Using the picture below, tell about George's neighborhood.

Singular/Plural

Nothing to Wear
Christmas Shopping

Nothing to Wear

Fred is upset this morning. He's looking for something to wear to work today, but there's nothing in his closet.

He's looking for a clean shirt, but all his shirts are dirty.

He's looking for a sport jacket, but all his sport jackets are at the dry cleaner.

He's looking for a pair of pants, but all the pants in his closet are ripped.

And he's looking for a pair of socks, but all his socks are on the clothes line, and it's raining!

Fred is having a difficult time this morning. He's getting dressed for work, but his closet is empty and there's nothing to wear.

1. Why is Fred upset?
2. Is there a clean shirt in Fred's closet?
3. Why not?
4. Is there a sport jacket?
5. Why not?
6. Is there a pair of pants for Fred to wear?
7. Why not?
8. Is there a pair of socks?
9. Why not?

Christmas Shopping

Mrs. Johnson is doing her Christmas shopping. She's looking for Christmas gifts for her family, but she's having a lot of trouble.

She's looking for a brown briefcase for her husband, but all the briefcases are black.

She's looking for a plain tie for her brother, but all the ties are fancy.

She's looking for a cotton blouse for her daughter, but all the blouses are polyester.

She's looking for an inexpensive necklace for her sister, but all the necklaces are expensive.

She's looking for a gray or brown raincoat for her father-in-law, but all the raincoats are yellow.

And she's looking for a leather pocketbook for her mother-in-law, but all the pocketbooks are plastic.

Poor Mrs. Johnson is very frustrated. She's looking for special gifts for all the special people in her family, but she's having a lot of trouble.

Good luck with your Christmas shopping, Mrs. Johnson! And Merry Christmas!

1. What's Mrs. Johnson doing?
2. Why is she having a lot of trouble?

Using the model below, tell a story about the laundromat. In your story, use some of the following words in the plural form.

blouse	pants	stocking
dress	sheet	sweater
jeans	shirt	tee shirt
nightgown	skirt	towel
pajamas	sock	undershirt

At the Laundromat

It's crowded at the laundromat today.

Mrs. Smith is washing her _towel_ and her _sheet_. Janet is drying her _blouse_ and her _pants_ Mr. and Mrs. Cramer are folding their _____ and their _____. And Jim is hanging up his _____ and his _____.

The owner of the laundromat is watching the people washing their clothes. He's very happy it's crowded at the laundromat today.

Mr. and Mrs. DiCarlo

Mr. and Mrs. DiCarlo

Mr. and Mrs. DiCarlo live in an old Italian neighborhood in New York City. They speak a little English, but usually they speak Italian.

They read the Italian newspaper. They listen to Italian radio programs. They shop at the Italian grocery store around the corner from their apartment building. And every day they visit their friends and neighbors and talk about life back in "the old country."

Mr. and Mrs. DiCarlo are upset about their son Joe. He lives in a small suburb outside the city, and he speaks very little Italian.

He reads American newspapers. He listens to American radio programs. He shops at big suburban supermarkets and shopping malls. And when he visits his friends and neighbors, he speaks only English.

In fact, the only time Joe speaks Italian is when he calls Mr. and Mrs. DiCarlo on the telephone or when he visits every weekend.

Mr. and Mrs. DiCarlo are sad because their son Joe speaks so little Italian. They're afraid he's forgetting his language, his culture, and his country.

1. Where do Mr. and Mrs. DiCarlo live?
2. How much English do they speak?
3. What language do they usually speak?
4. What do they read?
5. What do they listen to?
6. Where do they shop?
7. Who do they visit every day?
8. What do they talk about?
9. Who are Mr. and Mrs. DiCarlo upset about?
10. Why?
11. What does Joe read?
12. What does he listen to?
13. Where does he shop?
14. Who does he visit? What language does he speak?
15. When does Joe speak Italian?
16. Why are Mr. and Mrs. DiCarlo sad?

17. *What languages do the people in* YOUR *family speak?*

Mrs. Kowalski

Mrs. Kowalski lives in an old Polish neighborhood in Chicago. She's upset about her son Michael and his wife Kathy. Using the story on pages 48–50 as a model, tell a story about Mrs. Kowalski.*

* Retell the story on pages 48–50, but change "Mr. and Mrs. DiCarlo" to "Mrs. Kowalski," and change "Joe" to "Michael and Kathy."

Simple Present Tense: Negatives

10

Every Weekend Is Important to the Franklin Family

A Very Outgoing Person

Every Weekend Is Important
to the Franklin Family

Every weekend is important to the Franklin family. During the week they don't have very much time together, but they spend a LOT of time together on the weekend.

Mr. Franklin works at the shoe store downtown during the week, but he doesn't work there on the weekend.

Mrs. Franklin works at the city hospital during the week, but she doesn't work there on the weekend.

Bobby and Sally Franklin go to the elementary school during the week, but they don't go there on the weekend.

And the Franklins' dog Rover stays home alone during the week, but he doesn't stay home alone on the weekend.

On Saturday and Sunday the Franklins spend all their time together.

On Saturday morning they clean the house together. On Saturday afternoon they work in the garden together. And on Saturday evening they sit in the living room and watch TV together.

On Sunday morning they go to church together. On Sunday afternoon they have a big dinner together. And on Sunday evening they play their musical instruments together.

As you can see, every weekend is special to the Franklins. It's their only time together as a family.

1. Do the Franklins spend a lot of time together during the week?
2. When do they spend a lot of time together?
3. Where does Mr. Franklin work?
4. Does he work on the weekend?
5. When does he work?
6. Where does Mrs. Franklin work?
7. Does she work on the weekend?
8. When does she work?
9. Where do Bobby and Sally Franklin go to school?
10. Do they go to school on the weekend?
11. When do they go to school?
12. Where does the Franklins' dog Rover stay?
13. Does he stay home alone on the weekend?
14. When does he stay home alone?
15. What do the Franklins do on Saturday morning? on Saturday afternoon? on Saturday evening?
16. What do the Franklins do on Sunday morning? on Sunday afternoon? on Sunday evening?
17. Why is every weekend important to the Franklins?

18. *What do* you *do during the week?*
    What do you do on the weekend?

A Very Outgoing Person

Alice is a very outgoing person.

She spends a lot of time with her friends. She goes to parties. She goes to the movies. And she goes to discotheques. (She's very popular.)

She also likes sports very much. She plays basketball. She plays baseball. And she plays volleyball. (She's very athletic.)

Alice doesn't stay home alone very often. She doesn't read many books. She doesn't watch TV. And she doesn't listen to music. (She's very active.)

As you can see, Alice is a very outgoing person.

A Very Shy Person

Using the story on page 57 as a model, tell a story about Sheldon. Begin your story:

Sheldon is a very shy person. He doesn't spend a lot of time with his friends. He doesn't go. . . .

Tell about yourself.

What kind of person are you?
Are you outgoing? Are you shy?

How do you spend your time?
Do you like sports?
Do you stay home very much?
What do you do?

Object Pronouns
Simple Present Tense
Adverbs of Frequency

Close Friends

Close Friends

My husband and I are very lucky. We have many close friends in this city, and they're all interesting people.

Our friend Greta is an actress. We see her when she isn't making a movie in Hollywood. When we get together with her, she always tells us about her life in Hollywood as a movie star. Greta is a very close friend. We like her very much.

Our friend Dan is a scientist. We see him when he isn't busy in his laboratory. When we get together with him, he always tells us about his new experiments. Dan is a very close friend. We like him very much.

Our friends Bob and Carol are famous newspaper reporters. We see them when they aren't traveling around the world. When we get together with them, they always tell us about their conversations with presidents and prime ministers. Bob and Carol are very close friends. We like them very much.

Unfortunately, we don't see Greta, Dan, Bob, and Carol very often. In fact, we rarely see them because they're usually so busy. But we think about them all the time.

1. Why are they so lucky?
2. What does Greta do?
3. When do they see her?
4. What does she tell them about?
5. What does Dan do?
6. When do they see him?
7. What does he tell them about?
8. What do Bob and Carol do?
9. When do they see them?
10. What do they tell them about?
11. Why don't they see Greta, Dan, Bob, and Carol very often?

Tell about YOUR close friends.

What are their names?
Where do they live?
What do they do?
When do you get together with them?
What do you talk about?

**Contrast: Simple Present
and Present
    Continuous Tenses**

A Bad Day at the Office
Early Monday Morning
  in Centerville

A Bad Day at the Office

Mr. Blaine is the president of the Acme Insurance Company. His company is very large and always very busy.

Mr. Blaine has a staff of energetic employees who work for him. Unfortunately, all of his employees are out today. Nobody is there. As a result, Mr. Blaine is doing everybody's job, and he's having a VERY bad day at the office!

He's answering the telephone because the receptionist who usually answers the telephone is at the dentist's office.

He's typing letters because the secretary who usually types letters is home in bed with the flu.

He's operating the computer because the computer programmer who usually operates the computer is on vacation.

He's even fixing the radiator because the custodian who usually fixes the radiator is on strike.

Poor Mr. Blaine! It's a very busy day at the Acme Insurance Company, and nobody is there to help him. He's having a VERY bad day at the office!

1. What does Mr. Blaine do?
2. What kind of staff does he have?
3. Where are Mr. Blaine's employees today?
4. Who is there?
5. Why is Mr. Blaine answering the telephone?
6. Why is Mr. Blaine typing letters?
7. Why is Mr. Blaine operating the computer?
8. Why is Mr. Blaine fixing the radiator?

Early Monday Morning in Centerville

Early Monday morning is usually a very busy time in Centerville.

Men and women usually rush to their jobs. Some people walk to work. Some people drive. And others take the bus.

Children usually go to school. Some children walk to school. Some children take the school bus. And others ride their bicycles.

The city of Centerville is usually very busy. Trucks deliver food to the supermarkets. Mailmen deliver mail to homes and businesses. And policemen direct traffic at every corner.

Yes, early Monday morning is usually a very busy time in Centerville.

The Snowstorm

Using the story on pages 68–69 as a guide, complete the following story.

Today isn't a typical early Monday morning in Centerville. In fact, it's a very unusual morning. It's snowing very hard there. All the people are at home. The streets are empty. And the city is quiet.

The men and women who usually rush to their jobs aren't rushing to their jobs. The people who usually walk to work aren't walking to work. The people who usually drive aren't _____. And the people who usually take the bus aren't _____.

The children who usually go to school aren't _____. The children who usually _____. The children who usually _____. And the children who usually _____.

The city of Centerville is very quiet today. The trucks that usually _____. The mailmen who usually _____. And the policemen who usually _____.

Yes, it's a very unusual Monday morning in Centerville.

**Can
Have to**

The Ace Employment Service

Applying for a Driver's License

The Ace Employment Service

Roy, Susan, Lana, and Tina are sitting in the reception room at the Ace Employment Service. They're all looking for work, and they're hoping that the person they talk to today can help them.

Roy is looking for a job as a superintendent of an apartment building. He can paint walls. He can fix motors. And he can repair locks.

Susan is looking for a job as a secretary. She can type. She can file. And she can speak well on the telephone.

Lana and Tina are looking for jobs as actresses. They can sing. They can dance. And they can act.

Good luck, Roy! Good luck, Susan! Good luck, Lana and Tina! We hope you can find the jobs you're looking for.

1. Where are Roy, Susan, Lana, and Tina sitting?
2. Why?
3. What kind of job is Roy looking for?
4. What can he do?
5. What kind of job is Susan looking for?
6. What can she do?
7. What kinds of jobs are Lana and Tina looking for?
8. What can they do?

9. *What can YOU do?*

Applying for a Driver's License

Henry is annoyed. He's applying for a driver's license, and he's upset about all the things he has to do.

First he has to go to the Motor Vehicle Department and pick up an application form. He can't ask for the form by telephone, and he can't ask for it by mail. He has to go downtown and pick up the form in person.

He has to fill out the form in duplicate. He can't use a pencil. He has to use a pen. He can't use blue ink. He has to use black ink. And he can't write in script. He has to print.

He also has to attach two photographs to the application. They can't be old photographs. They have to be new. They can't be large. They have to be small. And they can't be black and white. They have to be color.

Then he has to submit his application. He has to wait in a long line to pay his application fee. He has to wait in another long line to have an eye examination. And believe it or not, he has to wait in ANOTHER long line to take a written test!

Finally, he has to take a road test. He has to start the car. He has to make a right turn, a left turn, and a U turn. And he even has to park his car on a crowded city street.

No wonder Henry is annoyed! He's applying for his driver's license, and he can't believe all the things he has to do.

1. Why is Henry annoyed?
2. What does he have to do first?
3. Can he ask for the form by telephone?
4. Can he ask for it by mail?
5. Where does he have to go?
6. How many copies of the form does he have to fill out?
7. Can he use a pencil?
8. Can he use blue ink?
9. Can he write in script?
10. What does he have to attach to the application form?
11. Can they be old?
12. Can they be large?
13. Can they be black and white?
14. Then how many long lines does he have to wait in? Why?
15. What does he have to do during the road test?

IN YOUR OWN WORDS

Explain how to apply for one of the following: a passport, a marriage license, a loan, college, or something else. In your explanation, use "you have to."*

* We usually use "you have to" to express "a person has to."

Future: Going to
Time Expressions

Happy New Year!
The Fortune-Teller

Happy New Year!

It's December thirty-first, New Year's Eve. Bob and Sally Simpson are celebrating the holiday with their children, Lucy and Tom. The Simpsons are a very happy family this New Year's eve. Next year is going to be a very good year for the entire family.

Next year, Bob and Sally are going to take a long vacation. They're going to visit Sally's cousin in California.

Lucy is going to finish high school. She's going to move to Boston and begin college.

Tom is going to get his driver's license. He's going to save a lot of money and buy a used car.

As you can see, the Simpsons are really looking forward to next year. It's going to be a happy year for all of them.

Happy New Year!

1. What day is it?
2. Why are the Simpsons happy this New Year's Eve?
3. What are Bob and Sally going to do next year?
4. What's Lucy going to do?
5. What's Tom going to do?

The Fortune-Teller

Walter is visiting Madame Sophia, the famous fortune-teller. He's very concerned about his future, and Madame Sophia is telling him what is going to happen next year.

According to Madame Sophia, next year is going to be a very interesting year in Walter's life.

In January he's going to meet a wonderful woman and fall in love.

In February he's going to get married.

In March he's going to take a trip to a warm, sunny place.

In April the weather is going to be very bad, and he's going to get the flu.

In May his parents are going to retire and move to California.

In June there's going to be a fire in his apartment building, and he's going to have to find a new place to live.

In July his friends are going to give him a radio for his birthday.

In August his boss is going to fire him.

In September he's going to start a new job with a very big salary.

In October he's going to be in a car accident, but he isn't going to be hurt.

In November he's going to be on a television game show and win a new car.

And in December he's going to become a father!

According to Madame Sophia, a lot is certainly going to happen in Walter's life next year. But Walter isn't sure he believes any of this. He doesn't believe in fortunes or fortune-tellers.

But in January he's going to get a haircut and buy a lot of new clothes, just in case Madame Sophia is right and he meets a wonderful woman and falls in love!

1. Who is Walter visiting?
2. What's he concerned about?
3. What's Madame Sophia telling him?
4. According to Madame Sophia, what's going to happen in January? in February? in March? in April? in May? in June? in July? in August? in September? in October? in November? in December?
5. Does Walter believe any of this?
6. What's he going to do, just in case?

IN YOUR OWN WORDS

Using the model below, tell about your plans for next week.

My Plans for Next Week

On Monday I'm going to _____.
On Tuesday I'm going to _____.
On Wednesday I'm going to _____.
On Thursday I'm going to _____.
On Friday I'm going to _____.
On Saturday I'm going to _____.
And on Sunday I'm going to _____.

Past Tense:
   Regular Verbs
   Introduction to
      Irregular Verbs

Preparing for a Party

The Wilsons' Party

Preparing for a Party

Mr. and Mrs. Wilson invited all their friends and neighbors to a party last night. They stayed home all day yesterday and prepared for the party.

In the morning the Wilsons worked outside. Their daughter Margaret cleaned the yard. Their son Bob painted the fence. Mrs. Wilson planted flowers in the garden, and Mr. Wilson fixed their broken front steps.

In the afternoon the Wilsons worked inside the house. Margaret washed the floors and vacuumed the living room carpet. Bob dusted the furniture and cleaned the basement. Mr. and Mrs. Wilson stayed in the kitchen all afternoon. He cooked spaghetti for dinner, and she baked apple pies for dessert.

The Wilsons finished all their work at six o'clock. Their house looked beautiful inside and out!

1. What did Margaret Wilson do in the morning?
2. What did Bob do?
3. What did Mrs. Wilson do?
4. What did Mr. Wilson do?
5. What did Margaret do in the afternoon?
6. What did Bob do?
7. What did Mr. and Mrs. Wilson do?

The Wilsons' Party

Everybody enjoyed the Wilsons' party last night. The guests arrived at about 7:30. After they arrived, they all sat in the living room. They ate cheese and crackers, drank wine, and talked.

Some people talked about their children. Other people talked about the weather. And EVERYBODY talked about how beautiful the Wilsons' house looked inside and out!

The Wilsons served dinner in the dining room at 9:00. Everybody enjoyed the meal very much. They liked Mr. Wilson's spaghetti, and they "loved" Mrs. Wilson's apple pie. In fact, everybody asked for seconds.

After dinner everybody sat in the living room again. First Bob Wilson played the piano and his sister Margaret sang. Then Mr. and Mrs. Wilson showed slides of their trip to Hawaii. After that, they turned on the stereo and everybody danced.

As you can see, the Wilsons' guests enjoyed the party very much. In fact, nobody wanted to go home!

1. What did the guests do after they arrived at the Wilsons' party?
2. What did they talk about?
3. What did the Wilsons do at 9:00?
4. Tell about the meal.
5. What did everybody do after dinner?
6. What did Bob do?
7. What did Margaret do?
8. What did Mr. and Mrs. Wilson do?
9. What did everybody do after that?

IN YOUR OWN WORDS

Tell about a party you enjoyed.

What did you eat?
What did you drink?
What did people do at the party?
    (eat, dance, talk about . . .)

Past Tense:
Yes/No Questions
WH Questions
More Irregular Verbs

Late for Work
Shirley's Day Off

Late for Work

Victor usually gets up at 7 a.m. He does his morning exercises for twenty minutes, takes a long shower, has a big breakfast, and leaves for work at 8 o'clock. He usually drives his car to work and gets there at 8:30.

This morning, however, he didn't get up at 7 a.m. He got up at 6 a.m. He didn't do his morning exercises for twenty minutes. He did them for only five minutes. He didn't take a long shower. He took a very quick shower. He didn't have a big breakfast. He had only a cup of coffee. He didn't leave for work at 8 o'clock. He left for work at 7.

Victor rushed out of the house an hour early this morning because his car is at the repair shop and he had to take the bus.

He walked a mile from his house to the center of town. He waited fifteen minutes for the bus. And after he got off the bus, he walked half a mile to his factory.

Even though Victor got up early and rushed out of the house this morning, he didn't get to work on time. He got there forty-five minutes late and his supervisor got angry and shouted at him.

Poor Victor! He really tried to get to work on time this morning.

1. Did Victor get up at 7 a.m. this morning?
2. When did he get up?

3. Did he do his morning exercises for twenty minutes?
4. How long did he do them?

5. Did he take a long shower?
6. What did he do?

7. Did he have a big breakfast?
8. What did he have?

9. Did he leave for work at 8 o'clock?
10. When did he leave for work?

11. Did Victor drive to work this morning?
12. Why not?
13. What did he have to take?

14. How far did he walk from his house to the center of town?
15. How long did he wait for the bus?
16. How far did he walk after he got off the bus?
17. Did Victor get to work on time?
18. How late did he get there?
19. What did his supervisor do?

Shirley's Day Off

Shirley enjoyed her day off yesterday. She got up late, went jogging in the park, came home, took a long shower, and had a big breakfast.

In the afternoon she went to the movies with her sister, and in the evening she had dinner with her parents. After dinner they sat in the living room and talked.

Shirley drove home at 10:00 and went to bed. She had a very pleasant day off yesterday.

IN YOUR OWN WORDS

Tell about a day off you enjoyed.

What did you do in the morning?
    in the afternoon? in the evening?

A Scary Night
Maria Gomez

A Scary Night

Louise was home alone last night for the first time. Nobody was there, and she was frightened.

Her brother Fred wasn't home. He was at a baseball game. Her brother Mike wasn't home. He was out on a date. Her parents weren't home either. They were at a meeting at her school.

Louise was afraid to be alone in the house. She decided to call her friends and invite them to come over and visit. Unfortunately, her friends weren't home. Not one of them!

She called her friend Patty, but Patty wasn't home. She was at the movies. She called her friend Melissa, but Melissa wasn't home. She was at the library. She called her friends Jane and Susan, but Jane and Susan weren't home either. They were at a concert.

Louise was very upset. Her family wasn't home. Her friends weren't home. Even her dog and her cat weren't home! They were across the street in the neighbor's yard.

What a scary night!

1. Why was Louise frightened?
2. Was her brother Fred home?
3. Where was he?
4. Was her brother Mike home?
5. Where was he?
6. Were her parents home?
7. Where were they?
8. What did Louise decide to do?
9. Was her friend Patty home?
10. Where was she?
11. Was her friend Melissa home?
12. Where was she?
13. Were her friends Jane and Susan home?
14. Where were they?
15. Were her dog and her cat home?
16. Where were they?

Maria Gomez

Maria Gomez was born in Peru. She grew up in a small village. She began school when she was six years old. She went to elementary school, but she didn't go to high school. Her family was very poor, and she had to go to work when she was thirteen years old. She worked on an assembly line in a shoe factory.

When Maria was seventeen years old, her family moved to the United States. First they lived in Los Angeles, and then they moved to San Francisco.

When Maria arrived in the United States, she was unhappy. She missed her friends back in Peru, and she didn't speak one word of English. She began to study English at night, and she worked in a factory during the day.

Maria studied very hard, and now she speaks English well. She's still studying at night, but now she's studying typing. She wants to be a secretary.

Maria still misses her friends back home. But she's very happy now, and she's looking forward to her future in her new country.

IN YOUR OWN WORDS

Tell a story about yourself or someone in your family. You can use some of these words in your story:

was born	moved
grew up	worked
began school	got married
studied	had children

CHAPTER-BY-CHAPTER WORD LIST

(n) = noun   (v) = verb

*indicates that the word or expression has not appeared in the corresponding chapter or previous chapters of *SIDE BY SIDE*.

1

What's Your Name? *2*

address
*apartment number
from
*I'm
is
*license number

*Mr.
*Mrs.
my
name
*nationality
phone number

*Social Security number
*telephone number
*what's
your

2

The Students in My English Class *7*

and
are
*Chinese
*countries
*different
*English class
*French
*friend
*friends
*Greek
he

he's
I
in
*interesting
*Japanese
*many
*Mexican
*Puerto Rican
*Russian
she
she's

*students
*tell about
the
they
they're
very
we're
what
where
yes

All the Students in My English Class Are Absent Today *9*

*absent
*all
*at
*dentist
*ever

*everybody
*everybody except me
home
hospital
*in bed

*our
*Social Security office
*today
*What a shame!

3

4

5

*friendly
*good
*having a few problems
having a terrible time
here
*hotel
How's the weather?
*in fact
isn't
*looking out the window
*love
*mother
new
old
*on
*other
playing cards
*raining cats and dogs
*repairman
restaurants
right now
*see you soon
sitting
*stomach
terrible
*to be
*together
*toilet
*to tell the truth
ugly
vacation
watching TV
*why
*writing (to)
you

IN YOUR OWN WORDS   26

big
classroom
*clean
difficult
easy
*friendly
handsome
heavy
*intelligent
large
*let
little
noisy
questions
quiet
*school building
*sincerely
small
thin
warm
*write back soon
young

6

Arthur Is Very Angry   29

*angry
*at night
*barking
*carpet
*clock
dancing
*having a big argument
*late
*looking at
*loud
*making a lot of noise
*man
*people
*practicing
*rock music
*teenagers
*vacuuming
*violin
*What a terrible night!
*Why not?
*woman

Tom's Wedding Day   30

*band
brother
champagne
crying
eating
father
favorite
fireplace
*getting to know each
  other
*grandparents
in front of
*in the corner
*politics
*popular music
*sentimental
sister
special
standing
*taking her photograph
*talking about
*"the good old days"
*wearing
wedding
*wedding cake
*wedding gown
*white
wife
*wonderful

7

The New Shopping Mall   *36*

*airport
*almost
 aren't
*because
*center of town
*city
*clothing stores
 department stores
 drugstore
*for

*men
*more than
 movie theater
 next to
 one hundred
*open
*outside
*owners
*shoe store
*shopping

*shopping mall
*some
*stores
*that
 there are
 there's
*toy store
*upset
 who
*women

Jane's Apartment Building   *39*

 across from
*all day and all night
 apartment building
 around the corner from
*convenient
 gas stations

 laundromat
*live
*near
 neighborhood
*noise
*place

*sidewalk
*there
*though
*walking

IN YOUR OWN WORDS

George's Apartment Building   *40*

 bus station

 clinic

 supermarket

8

Nothing to Wear   *43*

*closet
*clothes line
*dry cleaner
*empty
*getting dressed
 looking for

*nothing
 pair of
 pants
*ripped
 shirt
 socks

*something
*sport jacket
*this morning
*work

Christmas Shopping   *45*

 an
 black
 blouse
 briefcase

 brown
*Christmas shopping
*cotton
*crowded

 daughter
*father-in-law
*frustrated
*gifts

*good luck
gray
husband
*inexpensive
*leather

*Merry Christmas!
*mother-in-law
necklace
*plastic
pocketbook

*polyester
raincoat
*trouble
yellow

IN YOUR OWN WORDS

dress
*drying
*folding
*hanging up
*jeans

*nightgown
pajamas
*sheet
skirt
stocking

sweater
*tee shirt
*towel
*undershirt

9

*afraid
*a little English
*back in "the old
  country"
call on the telephone
*culture
do
does
every day
*forgetting

*grocery store
*how much
Italian
language
*life
*only
or
*radio programs
sad
*shop (at)

son
speak
*suburb
*suburban
*the only time
*usually
*visit
*weekend
*when

IN YOUR OWN WORDS

*Polish

10

*afternoon
*alone
*as a family
church

clean
dinner
doesn't
don't

*downtown
*during
*elementary school
*evening

*garden
go
have
*house

*important
*musical instruments
*on the weekend
Saturday

*spend time
*stay home
*time
*very much

A Very Outgoing Person   57

*active
*athletic
baseball
*basketball
discotheques

like
movies
*often
*outgoing
*parties

popular
sports
*volleyball

IN YOUR OWN WORDS
A Very Shy Person   58

*how
*shy

11

Close Friends   60

actress
*all the time
always
*close friends
*conversations
*experiments
*famous
*get together
him

*Hollywood
*laboratory
*making a movie
*movie star
presidents
prime-ministers
rarely
*reporters
*scientist

*see
*so
then
*think
*traveling around the
 world
*unfortunately
us

12

A Bad Day at the Office   67

*answer the telephone
*as a result
*computer
*computer programmer
*custodian
*dentist's office
*employees
*energetic
*flu

has
*help
*insurance company
*job
*letters
*nobody
*office
*on strike
*operate

*out
radiator
*receptionist
*secretary
*staff
*type
what kind of
*work for

14

Happy New Year!   *79*

*begin
*celebrating
 cousin
 December
*finish
*get
 going to

*Happy New Year!
*high school
*holiday
*looking forward to
*money
*New Year's Eve
 next year

 really
*take a vacation
*thirty-first
 this
*used car

The Fortune-Teller   *80*

*accident
 according to
*any of this
*become
*believe (in)
 boss
*certainly
 clothes
*concerned
*fall in love
*fire (n)
*fire (v)
*fortunes
*fortune-teller
*future

*game show
*get a haircut
*give
*happen
*just in case
*meet
*move
*parents
*retire
*right
*salary
*start
 sunny
 sure
*take a trip

*television
*win

 January
 February
 March
 April
 May
 June
 July
 August
 September
 October
 November
 December

IN YOUR OWN WORDS

My Plans for Next Week   *84*

*plans

 Monday

 Tuesday
 Wednesday
 Thursday

 Friday
 Saturday
 Sunday

15

Preparing for a Party   *86*

 apple pies
 bake
 basement
 broken
 cook
*dessert
*dust

*fence
 floors
*front steps
*furniture
*inside
*in the afternoon
*in the morning

 invite
 last night
 o'clock
*prepare for
*spaghetti
*stay
 work

The Wilsons' Party   88

*about 7:30
*after
*after that
 again
*arrive
*ask for seconds
 ate (eat)
*cheese

*crackers
 dining room
 drank (drink)
*enjoy
*guests
*love
*meal
 play the piano

 sat (sit)
*show
*stereo
*trip
*turn on
 want to
 wine

16

Late for Work   92

*an hour early
*coffee
*cup
 do exercises
*even though
*factory
 get up
 got (get)
*got (get) angry
*half a mile

*however
*how far
*how late
*how long
 leave
*left
*mile
*minutes
*on time
 poor

*repair shop
*rush out of the house
 shout (at)
*supervisor
*take a long shower
*take a quick shower
*try (to)
 wait for the bus

Shirley's Day Off   96

*came (come) home
*day off
*drove (drive)

 got (get) up
 had (have)
*pleasant

 took (take)
 went (go) jogging
*went (go) to bed

17

A Scary Night   98

 baseball game
*come over
 concert
*decide
*either

*for the first time
*frightened
 library
*meeting
*out on a date

*scary
 was
 wasn't
 were
 weren't

Maria Gomez   101

*assembly line
*back
 began (begin)
*born
*grew up (grow up)

*miss
 seventeen
*shoe factory
*still
 thirteen

*typing
*unhappy
*United States
*village
 years old

GENERAL WORD LIST

(adj) = adjective   (n) = noun   (v) = verb

The number after each word or expression indicates the page where it first appears.

A

a   15
about   88, 105
absent   9
accident   82
according to   80
across from   39
act   73
active   57
actress   60
address   2
afraid   50
after   89
afternoon   55
after that   89
again   89
airport   36
a little English   48
all   9
all day and all
   night   39
all the time   63
almost   37
alone   54
always   60
an   45
and   7
angry   29
an hour early   94
annoyed   74
another   75
answer the
   telephone   67
any of this   83
apartment   19
apartment
   building   39
apartment number   3
apple pie(s)   87
application fee   75

application form   74
apply(ing) for   74
April   81
are   7
aren't   37
around the corner
   from   39
arrive   88
as a family   55
as a result   67
ask for   74
ask for seconds   88
assembly line   101
as you can see   25
at   9
ate (eat)   88
athletic   57
at night   29
attach   74
August   82

B

back   101
back "in the old
   country"   48
bake   87
band   31
bark(ing)   29
baseball   57
baseball game   98
basement   87
basketball   57
bathroom   24
beach   16
beautiful   13
because   37
become   83
bed   23
began   101

begin   79
believe (in)   83
believe it or not   75
bicycle(s)   69
big   26
bird(s)   13
birthday party   34
black   45
blouse   45
blue   74
book   15
bored   23
born   101
boss   82
briefcase   45
broken   86
brother   32
brown   45
building   26
bus   68
business(es)   69
bus station   40
busy   19
but   22
by mail   74
by telephone   74

C

call on the
   telephone   50
came (come) home   96
can   73
car   19
carpet   29
celebrating
   (celebrate)   79
center of town   37
certainly   83